Silly Jokes for Kids!

By Silly Billy

Q: What does an evil hen lay?
A: Deviled eggs!

Q: What do you call cheese that's not your cheese?
A: Nacho cheese.

Q: What road has the most ghosts haunting it?
A: A dead end.
Q: What did the nut say when it sneezed?
A: Cashew!

Q: What does a mixed-up hen lay?
A: Scrambled eggs!

Q: Why was the cucumber mad?
A: Because it was in a pickle!

Q: What bird is with you at every meal?
A: A swallow!

Q: What do ghosts use to clean their hair?
A: Sham-boo!

Q: What did the baby corn say to the mama corn?

A: Where's pop?

Q: Why do monkeys like to eat bananas?

A: Because they have appeal!

Q: What do you call a shoe made from a banana?

A: A slipper!

Q: What do ghosts eat on Halloween?

A: Ghoulash!

Q: Why did the banana go to the doctor?
A: Because it wasn't peeling well.

Q: What do you get when a chicken lays an egg on top of a barn?
A: An eggroll!

Q: What did the skeleton order for dinner?
A: Spare ribs!

Q: Why did the cabbage win the race?
A: Because it was ahead!

Q: What do you call a cow with two legs?
A: Lean beef!

Q: What do you call a cow with no legs?
A: Ground beef!

Q: What cheese is made backwards?
A: Edam!

Q: What do sea monsters eat for lunch?
A: Fish and ships!
Q: How do chickens bake a cake?
A: From scratch!

Q: What room is useless for a ghost?
A: A living room!

Q: Why did Eeyore look in the loo?
A: Because he was looking for Pooh!!

Q: What do you call a bear with no teeth?
A: A gummy bear!

Q: If fruit comes from a fruit tree, where does chicken come from?
A: A poul-tree!

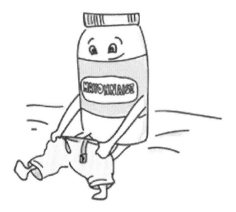

Q: What did the mayonnaise say when someone opened the refrigerator door?
A: Close the door, I'm dressing!

Q: Why do seagulls fly over the sea?
A: Because if they flew over the bay they would be called bagels!

Q: Why did the baker stop making doughnuts?
A: She was bored with the hole business!

Q: Why did the Cyclops stop teaching?
A: Because he only had one pupil

Q: Why couldn't the teddy bear eat his lunch?

A: Because he was stuffed!

Q: Where do tough chickens come from?

A: Hard-boiled eggs!

Q: What did the angry customer at the Italian restaurant give the chef?

A: A pizza of his mind!

Q: Why did the pig become an actor?

A: Because he was a ham!

Q: What did the burger name her daughter?
A: Patty!

CUSTOMER: Do you have spaghetti on the menu today?
WAITER: No, I cleaned it off.

Q: How do you fix a broken tomato?
A: With tomato paste!

Q: Why do dinosaurs eat raw meat?
A: Because they don't know how to cook!

Q: What do you get from a pampered cow?
A: Spoiled milk!

Q: How do you make a dinosaur float?
A: Put a scoop of ice cream in a glass of root beer and add one dinosaur!

Q: What weighs 800 pounds and sticks to the roof of your mouth?

15

A: A peanut butter and Stegosaurus
sandwich!

Q: Which is the left side of a pie?
A: The side that is not eaten!

Q: Why did the apple go out with a fig?
A: It couldn't find a date!

Q: What do little monsters eat?
A: Alpha-bat soup!

Q: What should you take on a trip to the desert?
A: A thirst-aid kit!

Patient: Doctor, I think I need glasses!
Waiter: You certainly do, this is a restaurant!

Q: What do polar bears eat for lunch?
A: Iceberg-ers!

Q: What's the best thing to put in a pie?
A: Your teeth!

Q: Waiter, will my pizza be long?
A: No sir, it will be round!

Q: What kind of vegetable would you like tonight?
A: Beets me!

Q: What happened to the cannibal who was late to dinner?
A: They gave her the cold shoulder!

Q: What is it called when a cat wins a dog show?
A: A cat-has-trophy.

Q: Why are graveyards noisy?
A: Because of all the coffin.

Q: What's the difference between a guitar and a fish?
A: You can't tune a fish.

Q: What do you call an alligator with a magnifying glass?
A: An investigator

Q: What do you get if you pamper a cow?

A: Spoiled milk.

Q: What do you get if you cross a fish and an elephant?
A: Swimming trunks.

Q: Where do bees go to the bathroom?
A: The BP station.

Q: Why did the bird go to hospital?
A: To get tweetment.

Q: What do you get when you cross a Labrador and a magician?

A: A labracadabrador!

Q: What do you call a sleeping bull?

A: A bulldozer.

Q: Why do sharks swim in saltwater?

A: Because pepper water makes them sneeze!

Q: What is a deer with no eyes called?

... No idea (eye-deer)

Q: What do you call a grizzly bear caught in the rain?

A: A drizzly bear!

Q: What color socks do bears wear?

They don't wear socks, they have bear feet!

Q: Why do hummingbirds hum?

A: Because they forgot the words!

Q: What did Dracula say about his girlfriend?

A: It was love at first bite!

Q: Did you hear the joke about the broken egg?
A: Yes, it cracked me up!

Q: What bird is with you at every meal?
A: A swallow!

Q: What bird is always sad?
A: The blue jay!

Q: Why didn't the zombie go to school?
A: He felt rotten!

Q: What is the biggest ant in the world?
A: An eleph-ant!

Q: Two flies are on the porch. Which one is an actor?
A: The one on the screen!

Q: Why was the baby ant confused?
A: Because all of his uncles were ants!

Q: What is even smarter than a talking bird?
A: A spelling bee!

Q: What do you get when you cross a walrus with a bee?
A: A wallaby!

Q: Why did the bee go to the doctor?
A: Because she had hives!

Q: What do you get if you cross a centipede and a parrot?
A: A walkie-talkie!

Q: What animal cheats at exams?
A: The cheetah!

Q: Why do you need a license for a dog and not for a cat?
A: Cats can't drive!

Q: What animals are the best pets?
A: Cats, because they are purr-fect!

Q: What kind of a key opens a banana?
A: A monkey!

Q: What did the banana say to the monkey?

A: Nothing, bananas can't talk!

Q: What does a cat on the beach have in common with Christmas?

A: Sandy claws!

Q: What did the ocean say when it saw the storm coming?

A: Nothing, it just waved.

Q: What season is it when you go on a trampoline?
A: Springtime.

Q: What do you call a sheep with no head or legs?
A: A cloud.

Q: What did the tornado say to the sports car?
A: Want to go for a spin!

Q: What kind of bow can't be tied?
A: A rainbow.

Q: What does a cloud wear under its raincoat?
A: Thunderwear.

Q: What do witches ask for at hotels?
A: Broom Service!.

Q: What did the tornado say to the other tornado?
A: Let's twist again like we did last summer.

Q: What's a tornado's favorite game?
A: Twister!

Q: What happens when it rains cats and dogs?
A: You might step in a poodle!

Q: Is it raining cats and dogs?
A: It's okay, as long as it doesn't rein-deer!

Q: Why is it cold on Christmas?
A: Because it's in Decembrrrr!

Q: Why is there a gate around cemeteries?
A: Because people are dying to get in!

Q: What did the lightning bolt say to the other lightning bolt?
A: You're shocking!

Q: What type of lightning likes to play sports?
A: Ball lightning!

Q: What sneaks around the kitchen on Christmas Eve?
A: Mince spies.
Q: What did the hurricane say to the other hurricane?
A: I have my eye on you!

Q: What's the difference between a horse and the weather?

A: One is reined up and the other rains down!

Q: Why did the woman go outdoors with her purse open?
A: Because she expected some change in the weather!

Q: What do you call it when it rains chickens and ducks?
A: Foul weather!

Q: What is Tarzan's favourite Christmas carol?

A: Jungle Bells.

Q: What do snowmen like to do after Christmas?
A: Chill out.

Q: Why didn't the turkey have any Christmas dinner?
A: Because he was stuffed.

Q: What did the cow say on December 25th?
A: Mooey Christmas!

Q: What did the snowman say to the other snowman?
A: Can you smell carrots?

Q: Why couldn't the Christmas tree stand up?
A: A Christmas tree does not have legs like we do!

Q: What is the most special part of your body at Christmas?
A: MistleTOE!

Q: What goes "oh, oh, oh"?
A: Santa walking backwards!

Q: What do monkeys sing at Christmas?
A: Jungle bells, jungle bells!

Q: What is green, white, and red all over?
A: A sunburnt elf!

Q: What rains at the north pole?
A: Reindeer!

Q: What do you get when you cross a teacher and a vampire?

A: A blood test!

Q: Where do snowmen keep their money?
A: In a snow bank.

Q: What does Santa say at the start of a race?
A: Ready, set, Ho! Ho! Ho!

Q: What's black and white and red all over?
A: A Newspaper!

Q: What happens when you throw a white hat into the Black sea?
A: It gets wet!

Q: What's black and white, black and white, and black and white?
A: A zebra caught in a revolving door!

Q: What's black and white, black and white, and black and white?
A: A panda bear rolling down a hill!

Q: What has one eye but cannot see?
A: A needle!

Q: What is black and white and red all over?
A: A randa with a sunburn!

Q: What is a black dog not a black dog?
A: When it's a grey-hound!

Q: What's orange and sounds like a parrot?
A: A carrot!

Q: What happened when a red ship crashed into a blue ship?
A: The crew was marooned!

Patient: I swallowed a lot of food coloring.
Doctor: You'll be okay.
Patient: But I feel like I've died inside!

Q: What's black and white, black and white, and black and white?
A: A penguin rolling down a hill!

Q: What do do when you find a blue elephant?
A: Cheer her up!

Q: What is gray and blue and very big?
A: An elephant holding its breath!

Q: What color is a ghost?
A: Boo!

Q: What's green and smells like blue paint?
A: Green paint!

Q: What do you do with a green monster?
A: Wait until she's ripe!

Q: What is a cat's favorite color?
A: Purr-ple!

Q: Why did the tomato turn red?
A: Because it saw the salad dressing!

Q: What color is a burp?
A: Burple!

Q: What's big and grey and protects you from the rain?
A: An umbrellaphant!

Q: What would you call the USA if everyone had a pink car?
A: A pink carnation!

Q: What is a cheerleader's favorite color?
A: Yeller!

Q: What's the most musical bone?
A: A trom-bone!

Q: What makes music on your head?
A: A head band!

Q: Why didn't the skeleton cross the road?
A: It didn't have the guts!

Q: What do you call a skeleton who won't work?
A: Lazy bones!

Q: What do elves learn in school?
A: The elfabet.

Q: What smells best at dinner?
A: Your nose.

Q: Which of Santa's reindeer has bad manners?
A: Rude-olph!

Q: What do you call witches who live together?

A: Broom-mates!

Q: Why is your nose in the middle of your face?

A: Because it is the scenter!

Q: How does a frog feel when he has a broken leg?
A: Unhoppy!

Q: What has no fingers, but many rings?
A: A tree!

Q: What do you call a dinosaur with no eyes?
A: Do-ya-think-he-saw-us!

**Q: What do you call a pirate with two eyes
and two legs?**
A: A rookie!

Q: Did you pick your nose?
A: No, I was born with it!

Q: What do you call a bear with no teeth?
A: A gummy bear!

Q: What did the left eye say to the right eye?
A: Something between us smells!

Q: What has eight legs and eight eyes?
A: Eight pirates!

Q: What kind of hair do oceans have?
A: Wavy!

Q: Why can't a nose be 12 inches long?
A: Because then it would be a foot!

Q: Why did the one-handed man cross the road?

A: To get to the second-hand shop!

Q: What do teddy bears do when it rains?

A: They get wet!

Q: Why shouldn't you tell a secret on a farm?

A: Because the potatoes have eyes and the corn has ears!

Q: What did the hurricane say to the other hurricane?

A: I have my eye on you!

Q: What do you call a fish without an eye?

A: fsh!

Q: Why couldn't the snake talk?

A: had a frog in his throat!

Q: What has a bottom at the top?

A: Your legs!

Q: Why are snakes hard to fool?
A: You can't pull their leg!

Q: Where do ghosts go when they're sick?
A: To the witch doctor!

Q: What position does a ghost play in soccer?
A: Ghoulie!

Q: What do you call a skeleton who won't work?
A: Lazy bones!

Q: What's a monster's favorite place to swim?
A: Lake Eerie!

Q: How do you make a skeleton laugh?
A: Tickle her funny bone!

Q: Why did the vampire flunk art class?
A: Because he could only draw blood!

Knock Knock!
Who's there?
Interrupting cow.
Interrupting-
MOO!!!!

Knock Knock!
Who's there?
Little old lady.
Little old lady who?
Wow, I didn't know you could yodel!

Knock Knock!
Who's there?
Boo.
Boo who?
Don't cry, it's only a joke.

Knock Knock!
Who's there?
Lettuce.
Lettuce who?
Lettuce in, it's freezing out here.

Knock Knock!
Who's there?
Bare.
Bare who?
Bare bum.

Knock Knock!
Who's there?
Wooden shoe.
Wooden shoe who?

Knock Knock!
Who's there?
Cow!

Cow who?
Cows don't go who, they go moo!

Knock Knock!
Who's there?
Atch.
Atch who?
Bless you.

Knock Knock!
Who's there?
Cash.
Cash who?
I knew you were a nut!

Knock Knock!
Who's there?
Isabell.
Isabell who?
Isabell working? I didn't hear anything.

Knock Knock!
Who's there?
Tank.
Tank who?
You're welcome

Knock Knock!
Who's there?
Smell mop.
Smell mop who?
Haha-you said smell my poo!

Knock Knock!
Who's there?
Doughnut.
Doughnut who?
Doughnut ask, it's a secret!

Knock Knock!
Who's there?
Broccoli.
Broccoli who?
Broccoli doesn't have a last name, silly.

Knock Knock!
Who's there?
Dishes.
Dishes who?
Dishes me, who are you?

Knock Knock!
Who's there?
Figs.
Figs who?
Figs the doorbell, it's broken!

Knock Knock!
Who's there?
Banana.
Banana who?
Knock Knock!
Who's there?
Orange.
Orange who?
Orange you glad I didn't say banana.

Knock Knock!
Who's there?
Orange.
Orange who?
Orange you glad I'm here.

Knock Knock!
Who's there?
Justin.
Justin who?
Justin time for lunch.

Knock Knock!
Who's there?
Olive.
Olive who?
Olive right next to you.

Knock Knock!
Who's there?
Olive.
Olive who?
Olive you.

THE END

These illustrations were sketched by myself.
If you'd like a copy of a PDF with all
illustration so you can spend hours of time
coloring in my artwork, for to the URL below
and fill out the form to receive the PDF free.

http://eepurl.com/c-R8xH

28407788R00037

Printed in Great Britain
by Amazon